The BUZZ on BEES

Why Are They Disappearing?

by **Shelley Rotner**
& Anne Woodhull

photographs by

Shelley Rotner

Holiday House / New York

One beautiful morning in 2006, professional beekeeper Dave Hackenberg went on a routine check of his hundreds of hives. But something was different.

Honeybees from a healthy hive

When he lifted the first cover, he discovered the hive was empty. As he continued lifting cover after cover, he was surprised to find that *all* of the hives were empty.

Dave listened for buzzing honeybees, but all he heard was silence. There were no bees. There were no dead bees either.

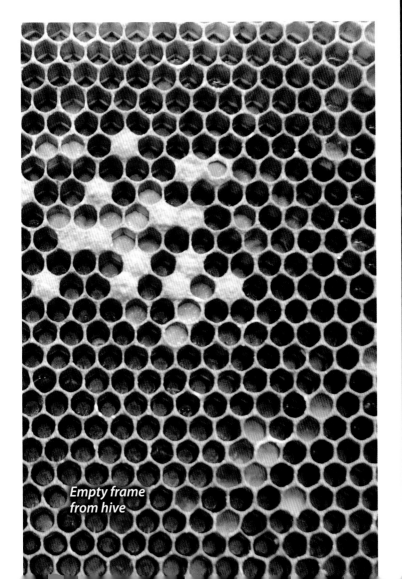

Empty frame from hive

Beekeeper at hive

"I've been a beekeeper for over fifty years, and I've never seen anything like it," Dave said. "I came to pick up four hundred hives and discovered thousands of bees had just flat-out disappeared."

Dave with hives

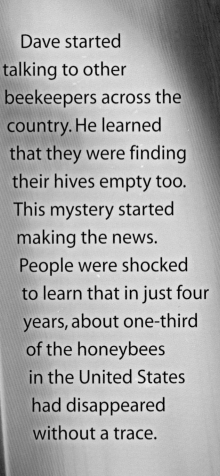

Dave started talking to other beekeepers across the country. He learned that they were finding their hives empty too. This mystery started making the news. People were shocked to learn that in just four years, about one-third of the honeybees in the United States had disappeared without a trace.

Why is the loss of something as small as a honeybee such a big deal?
We know that honeybees make honey, but we can live without honey. However, honeybees do something much more important. They pollinate.

Pollen is a yellow powder found in flowers, and sometimes it can make you sneeze. It is necessary to help grow new plants. As a honeybee buzzes from flower to flower, collecting nectar to make honey, grains of pollen stick to its body. When the bee lands on another flower, some of the pollen rubs off.
This process is called pollination. When a plant is pollinated, it can make new plants. Bees help deliver pollen so that pollination can happen.

Native bees, known as "wild bees," pollinate too and are also disappearing. Unlike honeybees that work in a hive, most native bees work on their own. They make individual nests, usually in trees, under the ground, or in leaf stems.

Honeybee collecting pollen

In order for a strawberry plant to grow strawberries, or an apple tree to grow apples, pollen needs to be transferred from one plant to another. Honeybees and other bees help deliver the pollen so that pollination can happen.

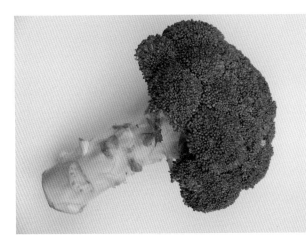

Honeybees are master pollinators. We can thank them for about one out of every three mouthfuls of food that we eat.

Without bees, but especially without honeybees, there would be fewer cantaloupes, cucumbers, blueberries, peppers, broccoli, soybeans, watermelons, peaches, tomatoes, pumpkins, onions, and almonds. So many of the fruits, nuts, and vegetables we eat depend on honeybees for pollination.

Honeybees also pollinate the cotton plants we need to make our shirts and jeans. And they pollinate clover, which is eaten by sheep, cows, and goats. These animals provide us with meat and milk. From milk we make cheese and butter.

Bees are not the only pollinators. Birds and bats pollinate. So do beetles and other insects. Ponds, lakes, rivers, and a good rain shower can also carry pollen from one plant to another. So can wind.

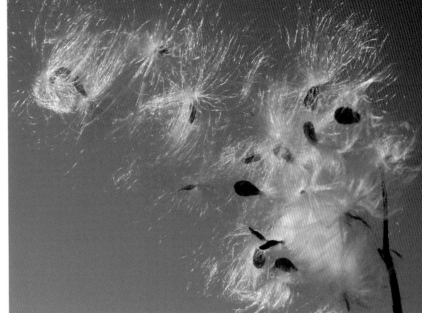

Honeybees are the most important bees in modern agriculture. Their massive workforce pollinates the largest variety of crops. They are easy to manage and easy to move. Some leave their hives and survive on their own.

Besides honeybees, there are more than four thousand species of native bees in North America that pollinate as well. Some of these bees are especially good at pollinating specific crops.

Honeybees working in a healthy hive and surrounding a queen

The *bumblebee* has an extra-hairy coat so it can collect nectar on cold days. It lives in a small colony and is the only pollinator of the potato flower.

Carpenter bees chew perfectly round holes in wood to make nests to raise their young. They are excellent pollinators of eggplants and tomatoes.

Leaf-cutter bees (right) make their nests by cutting leaves. Using round pieces of leaves, they seal the holes that are filled with eggs, nectar, and pollen.

Mining bees make holes in the ground from one inch to several feet deep. They put eggs, nectar, and pollen at the end of these holes and seal them until the new bees are born.

The *sweat bee* (right) likes to land on your skin and lick the salt there but will not sting unless provoked. It helps pollinate blueberry and watermelon plants.

Besides pollinating
many plants in the wild,
honeybees help pollinate more
than ninety different kinds of crops
on both small and large farms.

The MacLaurys in Vermont are beekeepers
on a fairly small scale. They have about twenty-five
hives. They raise bees primarily for their honey, but
they also make beeswax candles and honey soaps. Their bees
pollinate flowers and vegetables within five miles of their hives.

*A small farm
in Vermont*

The MacLaurys examine their bees.

Larger farms, made up of hundreds of acres, usually grow only one crop and need thousands of hives. Beekeepers such as Dave Hackenberg transport their bees all over the country to pollinate these large crops.

Beekeepers wear protective suits so they don't get stung as they load the hives onto huge flatbed trucks. This happens in the cool of the evening when the bees return to their hives to rest. The bees are then moved from place to place and job to job, following crops as they bloom.

Dave loading bees

A truckload of Pennsylvania bees might start by pollinating almonds in California, then travel back across the country to pollinate apples in New York, blueberries in Maine, and pumpkins in New Jersey. New York's apple crop requires 30,000 hives, Maine's blueberry crop needs 50,000 hives, and California's almond crop requires 1½ million hives. Each hive is home to between 10,000 and 60,000 honeybees.

At different times in history, beekeepers have reported losses, but nothing as widespread as the decline in honeybees since 2004. Scientists call this Colony Collapse Disorder, or CCD.

Beekeepers and scientists are working together to solve this mystery. They are examining healthy and sick bees to try and figure out why bees are more fragile today than in the past.

Bees in a healthy hive

A hive
with CCD

What are the factors causing honeybees to disappear?

Most research has been done on honeybees, but native bees have been declining as well. There are many theories, but no one knows for sure. Since honeybees have a delicate immune system, most beekeepers and scientists agree their health can be affected by many factors.

Are honeybees in a weakened state, unable to fight off disease? They are becoming sick with a variety of ailments caused by viruses, bacteria, fungi, and parasites such as the varroa mite.

Are honeybees getting sick from contact with other bees? Honeybees are often shipped from place to place. Are they exposed to new diseases that they take home and spread to local bees? Can bees shipped from other countries bring new diseases as well?

Is long-distance transporting putting too much stress on the bees? Perhaps when bees are enclosed while traveling in trucks, they do not get enough water or cannot regulate the temperature in their hives. They are easily affected by changes in temperature, and there are big temperature changes between Maine and California.

How do drugs affect the health of honeybees? Some honeybees are given antibiotics to help prevent diseases. This helps them fight infection, but can it cause them to lose important bacteria they need to digest food?

What about diet? Some honeybees are fed sugar water and corn syrup as supplements or substitutions for their natural diet. How does this affect their health?

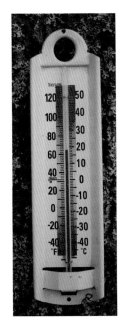

What about the loss of habitat? With urban development there is less vegetation. Bees are losing some of their food sources. When large farms keep expanding, planting acres of one kind of plant, we lose plant diversity. How will bees find well-balanced sources of food?

What about global warming? Rising temperature changes can mean that there is less water and food available for bees. Where will bees thrive?

What about air pollution? We know that people's health can be affected by air pollution. What effect does this have on bees? Does pollution also affect the ability of bees to find the fragrance of flowers?

What about electromagnetic fields? Do cell phones and cell towers interfere with bees' navigation systems, causing them to lose their way back to their hives?

What about chemicals? Pesticides are often sprayed on crops to kill insects. Honeybees are insects too. Are they being poisoned by their contaminated food sources? Many chemicals used for fertilization have leached and mixed into our soil and water. Are the bees' immune and navigation systems affected by ingesting these chemicals?

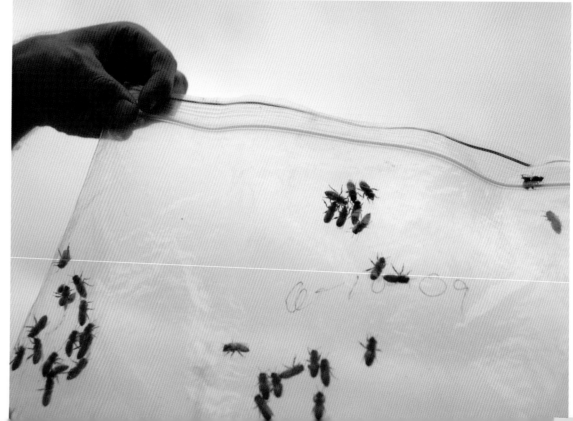

What are scientists doing to help solve this mystery?
Some are investigating native and imported bees to see
if they are more disease resistant and adaptive
to the environment. If so, these bees might
help do the jobs that honeybees do.

Others are studying environmental
factors that might compromise
the survival of the honeybee,
including the effects of global
changes as well as
manufactured chemicals
and pesticides.

Some believe that
honeybees are
disappearing because
they catch viruses such
as the flu or other diseases
and become too weak to
recover. Scientists have been
feeding honeybees
supplemental vitamins to see if
this can help strengthen their immune
systems and general health.

*Bee with cranberry
blossom under
microscope*

The mystery of the disappearing bees may be a warning. Different kinds of bees have been on Earth for more than 65 million years—since the days of the dinosaurs. But now bees are in trouble, their future unknown. When so many honeybees begin to disappear, we have to ask the bigger question: how healthy is our earth?

Bees, just like us, need good food, clean water, and clean air to stay healthy. All life depends on many parts working together. Bees are small, but they can make a big difference in our large world.

Honeybee

What can we do?

"Bee" active! There is so much we can do!

Encourage your parents to become beekeepers! This will help keep the honeybee population growing.

Ask your family and friends to support local beekeepers and to buy locally grown foods, which don't have to be trucked long distances. This cuts down on pollution by using less fuel and producing fewer emissions.

Plant a vegetable garden. There will be more flowering plants to feed bees. Local gardens cut down the need to transport food. This cuts down on pollution and fuel consumption.

Support local beekeepers. Use honey instead of sugar. It is the most environmentally friendly and healthy sweetener.

Plant a bee garden. Some flowers that bees especially like are black-eyed Susans, California poppies, forget-me-nots, sunflowers, and coneflowers.

Encourage your parents to buy foods that are grown organically (without chemicals and insecticides).

Plant meadows instead of lawns. Plan and organize with your community to create "wildscapes" in public places. Not only will you help feed bees, but also your town will look more beautiful.

Avoid spraying pesticides to control weeds and insects.

Plant flowers that will bloom at different times so that your bees will have food all summer long.

Invite your local beekeeping organization to speak at your school.

Talk to your friends, your class, and your community to spread the word that bees need help now!

Find out more!

Here are some resources to check out.

ABC and XYZ of Bee Culture by A. I. Root and E. R. Root (Medina: Kissinger Publishing, 2005). An encyclopedia of information about honeybees and beekeeping. First published in 1877 and added to and republished many times.

The Bumblebee Pages: www.bumblebee.org. A site mostly about bumblebees and some other bees as well.

Discover Life: www.discoverlife.org. This website includes information about "Bee Hunt," a study inviting students and other volunteers to investigate factors that have an impact on plant-pollinator interactions.

Hives for Lives: www.hivesforlives.com. After their grandfather died from throat cancer, two girls, ages ten and twelve, started selling honey and donated the proceeds to help find a cure. Five years later, they have raised more than $150,000 and have become bee experts.

Honey Files: www.honey.com/consumers/kids/honeyfiles.asp. A video and educational guide for grades 4–6 about bees, honey, and pollination. Sponsored by the National Honey Board.

The Honeybee Project: www.thehoneybeeproject.com. Children's educational project to raise awareness about honeybees.

Meetmeatthecorner.org: David Graves's video teaches children about city beekeeping.

Pollinator Partnership: www.pollinator.org. Dedicated to protecting the health of pollinators across North America.

Spikenard Farm: www.spikenardfarm.org. A biodynamic farm with holistic beekeeping at its center, Spikenard experiments with organic methods and solutions to bee-raising problems.

Urban Bee Gardens: www.nature.berkeley.edu/urbanbeegardens. An excellent site on bees in gardens.

The Xerces Society for Invertebrate Conservation: www.xerces.org. Fact sheets and information about what you can do to help bees.

Learn about different corporations and organizations that are helping to raise awareness and fund research, such as Häagen-Dazs, Burt's Bees, and Wyman's Blueberries.

Did you know?

Honeybees have a dancing language. They dance to let other bees know the location of flowers.

Bumblebees buzz a high vibrational sound in the range of middle C.

Bees fly more than twelve miles an hour going forward. They can fly backward and sideways too.

A bee can visit ten flowers a minute.

Bees have two pairs of wings that flap 250 times a second.

Bees have two different kinds of eyes: one set allows them to see ultraviolet markings on the blossom, which helps direct them to the nectar. Another set of three eyes on top of their forehead allows them to see the sun, even on a cloudy day.

Honeybees collect nectar from more than a million flowers to make one pound of honey.

Honey is thought to cure many ailments. Since bacteria does not grow in honey, it has been used since ancient times to dress wounds and burns. Some believe honey helps to heal sore throats and relieve fever.

A beehive was put on the south lawn of the White House in 2009. It is thought to be the first one ever put there and is tended by beekeeper Charlie Brandts.

We dedicate our book to all those who take action to protect, preserve, and sustain our world.
Special thanks to our bee experts. They have shared facts, research, observations,
and their passion to help solve the mystery of the disappearing bees.

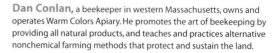

John Burand is a professor of plant, soil, and insect sciences and microbiology at the University of Massachusetts. He is a member of the University of Massachusetts Amherst Bee Consortium, which received a grant from the U.S Department of Agriculture to research and improve the health of both honeybees and bumblebees.

Dan Conlan, a beekeeper in western Massachusetts, owns and operates Warm Colors Apiary. He promotes the art of beekeeping by providing all natural products, and teaches and practices alternative nonchemical farming methods that protect and sustain the land.

Dave Hackenberg has been a beekeeper for forty-seven years and operates three thousand colonies of honeybees for honey, beeswax, and pollination services. He was president of the Beekeeping Federation for two years and a member for twenty-five. When he discovered the massive die-offs in his hives, his persistence in finding the reason began the nationwide search for an answer.

Steven and **Carol MacLaury** are beekeepers in Weston, Vermont. They tend to two million bees and twenty-eight hives. They make beeswax candles, honey soaps, and creamed and raw honey products. They are happy beekeepers, endlessly inspired by their bees.

Dennis van Englesdorp has been passionate about bees his whole life. He is the state apiarist of Pennsylvania and does scientific research at Penn State. He and other researchers took Dave Hackenberg's concerns seriously, began work, and named this problem Colony Collapse Disorder. *Photo by Ellen Harasimowicz*

Marla Spivak is Professor and Extension Entomologist in the Department of Entomology at the University of Minnesota. Her research and extension efforts focus on honeybee health, breeding, and behavior, and on the sustainable management of alternative pollinators. *Photo by Michael Simone*

Matthew Shepherd is the senior conservation associate of The Xerces Society for Invertebrate Conservation. He works with people from all walks of life to promote awareness about and protection of pollinators. *Photo by Karen Shepherd*

"Stop and think about how many ways pollinators touch our daily routines—from the milk at breakfast to the apple in your lunch box to the cotton clothes you wear—and you realize how important it is to find ways to protect bees, butterflies, flies, beetles, and other insects that provide us with the service of pollination."
Matthew Shepherd

A special thanks to Susan Pearson, David Graves, Hans Tensma, Hans Leo,
Eric Eaton, Craig Hollingsworth, Al Card, Claire Counihan, Eleni Beja, and Gordon Thorne

*The publisher wishes to thank Louis Sorkin, entomologist at the American Museum
of Natural History, for reviewing this book for accuracy.*

Library of Congress Cataloging-in-Publication Data
The buzz on bees : why are they disappearing? / by Shelley Rotner and Anne Woodhull ; photographs by Shelley Rotner. — 1st ed.
p. cm.
ISBN 978-0-8234-2247-0 (hardcover)
1. Colony collapse disorder of honeybees—Juvenile literature. 2. Honeybee—Juvenile literature. I. Woodhull, Anne Love. II. Title.
SF538.5.C65R68 2010
638'.1—dc22
2009024208